Valde Books

www.valdebooks.com - 2009

The Calvary Road

by

Roy Hession

Contributors:

Revel Hession

TABLE OF CONTENTS

INTRODUCTION

By NORMAN P. GRUBB, Hon. Secretary of the Worldwide Evangelization Crusade, London

I am sure from my own experience, as well as from what we have seen in the ranks of our Mission these last three years, that what the authors tell us about in these pages is one of God's vital words to His worldwide church today. For long I had regarded revival only from the angle of some longed for, but very rare, sudden outpouring of the Spirit on a company of people. I felt that there was a missing link somewhere. Knowing of the continuing revival on a certain mission field, and because it was continuing and not merely sudden and passing, I long felt that they had a further secret we needed to learn. Then the chance came for heart-to-heart fellowship with them, first through one of our own missionary leaders whose life and ministry had been transformed by a visit to that field, and then through conferences with some of their missionaries on furlough and finally through the privilege of having two of the native brethren living for six months at our headquarters.

From them I learned and saw that revival is first personal and immediate. It is the constant experience of any simplest Christian who "walks in the light," but I saw that walking in the light means an altogether new sensitiveness to sin, a calling things by their proper name of sin, such as pride, hardness, doubt, fear, self-pity, which are often passed over as merely human reaction. It means a readiness to "break" and confess at the feet of Him who was broken for us, for the Blood does not cleanse excuses, but always cleanses sin, confessed as sin; then revival is just the daily experience of a soul full of Jesus and running over.

Further, we are beginning to learn, as a company of Christ's witnesses, that the rivers of life to the world do not flow out in their fulness through one man, but through the body, the team. Our brokenness and openness must be two-way, horizontal as well as vertical, with one another as with God. We are just beginning to experience in our own ranks that team work in the Spirit is one of the keys to revival, and that we have to learn and practice the laws of a living fellowship.

I need not say more, as Roy Hession and his wife expound the whole matter. But we have seen God at work in our midst. I could name half-a-dozen of our workers, several of them leaders, in whose lives there has been a new spiritual revolution. Then rivulets of blessing in some of our individual lives have been merging in a larger stream. God has been giving us times as a company when "as they prayed, the place was shaken where they were assembled together, and they were all filled with the Holy Ghost." Here and there on our battle fields, distant and near, the sound of abundance of rain is being heard; and we believe among many companies of

God's people He is preparing afresh for these last days a "sharp threshing instrument having teeth," and that what God is saying to us through this Revival, and through the interpretation of that message in this pamphlet, is a word of the Lord for our day. May it be greatly used to produce revived lives, revived fellowships and revived churches.

PREFACE

In April, 1947, several missionaries came at my invitation to an Easter Conference which I was organising. I invited them to come as speakers, because I had heard that they had been experiencing Revival in their field for a number of years, and I was interested in Revival. What they had to say was very different from much of what I had associated with Revival. It was very simple and very quiet. As they unfolded their message and gave their testimonies, I discovered that I was the neediest person in the conference and was far more in need of being revived than I had ever realised. That discovery, however, only came slowly to me. Being myself one of the speakers, I suppose I was more concerned about others' needs than my own. As my wife and others humbled themselves before God and experienced the cleansing of the precious Blood of Jesus, I found myself left somewhat high and dry--dry just because I was high. I was stumbled by the simplicity of the message, or rather the simplicity of what I had to do to be revived and filled with the Spirit. When others at the end of the conference testified of how Jesus had broken them at His Cross and filled their hearts to overflowing with His Holy Spirit, I had no such testimony. It was only afterwards that I was enabled to give up trying to fit things into my doctrinal scheme, and come humbly to the Cross for cleansing from my own personal sins. It was like beginning my Christian life all over again. My flesh "came again like that of a little child," as did Naaman's when he was willing to humble himself and dip himself in Jordan. And it has been an altogether new chapter in life since then. It has meant, however, that I have had to choose constantly to die to the big "I," that Jesus might be all, and constantly to come to Him for cleansing in His precious Blood. But that is just why it is a new chapter.

At that time my wife and I had been issuing a little paper which we called "Challenge," in which we were seeking to lead young Christians into a deeper experience of the Lord Jesus. It was natural, then, that in the following issue we should put down what God had shown us. We simply put down in print the Message of Revival as it had come to us. There was a sudden and surprising demand for the little paper, because it carried this simple message. As we continued to write further of the Message of Revival in subsequent issues, the demand continued to increase surprisingly. Letters came in almost every day telling of the way God was blessing His people through it, and asking for further supplies. Requests began to come from far away countries, to which the little paper was finding its way, and news began to come of the beginnings of revival in the lives of God's people in various parts. Translations too were made into French and German. We had been caught up in the current of God's working beyond anything we expected or deserved. Indeed we had nothing to glory in, for it became evident that revival blessing was not so much the result of "Challenge," as that "Challenge" was the result of revival blessing. God was at work in many hearts and in many parts. The testimony of those who had been revived made others hungry, who in turn found their way to the Cross, and so the blessing spread from life to life. And wherever the blessing spread, the little paper seemed to go, for it sought to put in clear and Scriptural language what so many were beginning to experience.

The connection of all this with the present little book is that this book is simply a collection of some of those numbers of "Challenge." Circumstances make it difficult at the moment for us to continue to send out further issues of "Challenge," and yet the requests for back numbers have continued to come in. There is obviously a need for this simple Message of Revival to be made available to a wider circle of readers, for there is a growing thirst in God's people for the Rivers of Living Water. And so, encouraged by God's blessing on what has gone before, we have put together some of the more helpful numbers of "Challenge," together with two extra chapters, and send them on their way, looking to God to use them as He will. We cannot boast that this contains an orderly treatment of our subject chapter by chapter. Each article was designed to be complete in itself, and therefore now that they are put together in one pamphlet, there cannot but be a good deal of overlapping, and certain things will be seen to be repeated again and again. It cannot, therefore, be regarded as an ordinary book, and the chapters might best be read each one on its own, rather than the whole of them at one sitting.

It must not be thought that this pamphlet represents a purely personal contribution on our part. The things recorded in this book have been learnt in fellowship with others in various parts, who have begun, like ourselves, to walk the Way of the Cross in a new way. Any others in that fellowship might have written these chapters. It is a fellowship, too, which is continually growing, for an ever-increasing number of lives are being quietly influenced and blessed by the movement of Revival in this country now. This fact, we think, adds to the strength and significance of what is here written.

Now a word about Revival itself. The conception of Revival contained in the following pages may come as a surprise to many. The common conception of Revival is usually that of a spectacular religious awakening, in which large numbers of the unconverted are convicted of sin and brought to Christ amid a good deal of excitement. Such a visitation of God's Spirit, while greatly to be desired, is thought to be largely unaccountable. It is something for which one can only pray and we must wait for it in God's good time. Meantime we must go on being defeated and the Church must somehow contrive to continue her witness without New Life. Some of us are finding in actual fact that true revival is often the very reverse of all this. Revival need not be spectacular at all (it is certainly no spectacle to the one who is facing up to his sins in the light of the Cross!). Indeed where there is evidence of the spectacular, it is often the least important part of revival. Our missionary friends seemed studiously to avoid reference to the spectacular side of what they had been through, lest it might obscure the real challenge of what God was saying to us. Then, too, revival is not something that God does firstly among the unconverted, but among His people. Revival simply means New Life, and that implies that there is already Life there, but that the Life has ebbed. The unconverted do not need revival, for there is not any life there to revive. They need vival. It is the Christians who need revival. But that presupposes that there has been a declension. You only revive that which has grown weak. And they only are candidates for revival who are prepared to confess that there has been a declension in their lives. And the more specific the confession, the more definitely will God revive. And when that happens among us Christians, God will be able to work among the lost in new power and we shall see a new work of grace there. One of Evan Roberts' mottoes in the days of the Welsh Revival was "Bend the Church and save the people." And the two are always linked. The world has lost its faith, because the Church has lost its fire.

One last thing needs to be said about the necessary attitude of heart of the reader. If God is to bless him at all through these pages, he must come to them with a deep hunger of heart. He must be possessed with a dissatisfaction of the state of the Church in general, and of himself in particular--especially of himself. He must be willing for God to begin His work in himself first, rather than in the other man. He must, moreover, be possessed with the holy expectancy that God can and will meet his need. If he is in any sense a Christian leader, the urgency of the matter is intensified many times over. His willingness to admit his need and be blessed will determine the degree to which God can bless the people to whom he ministers. Above all he must realise that he must be the first to humble himself at the Cross. If a new honesty with regard to sin is needed among his people, he must realise it must begin with himself. It was when the King of Nineveh arose from his throne and covered himself with sackcloth and sat in ashes as a sign of his repentance, that his people repented.

Let not, however, those readers who are not leaders be tempted to look at those who are and wait for them. God wants to begin with each one of us. He wants to begin with YOU.

May God bless us all.

Roy HESSION. January, 1950.

CHAPTER I.

BROKENNESS

We want to be very simple in this matter of Revival. Revival is just the life of the Lord Jesus poured into human hearts. Jesus is always victorious. In heaven they are praising Him all the time for His victory. Whatever may be our experience of failure and barrenness, He is never defeated. His power is boundless. And we, on our part, have only to get into a right relationship with Him, and we shall see His power being demonstrated in our hearts and lives and service, and His victorious life will fill us and overflow through us to others. And that is Revival in its essence.

If, however, we are to come into this right relationship with Him, the first thing we must learn is that our wills must be broken to His will. To be broken is the beginning of Revival. It is painful, it is humiliating, but it is the only way. It is being "Not I, but Christ,"[footnote1:Gal. 2: 20.] and a "C" is a bent "I." The Lord Jesus cannot live in us fully and reveal Himself through us until the proud self within us is broken. This simply means that the hard unyielding self, which justifies itself, wants its own way, stands up for its rights, and seeks its own glory, at last bows its head to God's will, admits its wrong, gives up its own way to Jesus, surrenders its rights and discards its own glory--that the Lord Jesus might have all and be all. In other words it is dying to self and self-attitudes.

And as we look honestly at our Christian lives, we can see how much of this self there is in each of us. It is so often self who tries to live the Christian life (the mere fact that we use the word "try" indicates that it is self who has the responsibility). It is self, too, who is often doing Christian work. It is always self who gets irritable and envious and resentful and critical and worried. It is self who is hard and unyielding in its attitudes to others. It is self who is shy and self-conscious and reserved. No wonder we need breaking. As long as self is in control, God can do little with us, for all the fruits of the Spirit (they are enumerated in Galatians 5), with which God longs to fill us, are the complete antithesis of the hard, unbroken spirit within us and presupposes that it has been crucified.

Being broken is both God's work and ours. He brings His pressure to bear, but we have to make the choice. If we are really open to conviction as we seek fellowship with God (and willingness for the light is the prime condition of fellowship with God), God will show us the expressions of this proud, hard self that cause Him pain. Then it is, we can stiffen our necks and refuse to repent or we can bow the head and say, "Yes, Lord." Brokenness in daily experience is simply the response of humility to the conviction of God. And inasmuch as this conviction is continuous, we shall need to be broken continually. And this can be very costly, when we see all the yielding of rights and selfish interests that this will involve, and the confessions and restitutions that may be sometimes necessary.

For this reason, we are not likely to be broken except at the Cross of Jesus. The willingness of Jesus to be broken for us is the all-compelling motive in our being broken too. We see Him, Who is in the form of God, counting not equality with God a prize to be grasped at and hung on to, but letting it go for us and taking upon Him the form of a Servant--God's Servant, man's Servant. We see Him willing to have no rights of His own, no home of His own, no possessions of His own, willing to let men revile Him and not revile again, willing to let men tread on Him and not retaliate or defend Himself. Above all, we see Him broken as He meekly goes to Calvary to become men's scapegoat by bearing their sins in His own body on the Tree. In a pathetic passage in a prophetic Psalm, He says, "I am a worm and no man."[footnote2:Psalm 22: 6.] Those who have been in tropical lands tell us that there is a big difference between a snake and a worm, when you attempt to strike at them. The snake rears itself up and hisses and tries to strike back--a true picture of self. But a worm offers no resistance, it allows you to do what you like with it, kick it or squash it under your heel--a picture of true brokenness. And Jesus was willing to become just that for us--a worm and no man. And He did so, because that is what He saw us to be, worms having forfeited all rights by our sin, except to deserve hell. And He now calls us to take our rightful place as worms for Him and with Him. The whole Sermon on the Mount with its teaching of non-retaliation, love for enemies and selfless giving, assumes that that is our position. But only the vision of the Love that was willing to be broken for us can constrain us to be willing for that.

"Lord, bend that proud and stiff necked I,

Help me to bow the head and die;

Beholding Him on Calvary,

Who bowed His head for me."

But dying to self is not a thing we do once for all. There may be an initial dying when God first shows these things, but ever after it will be a constant dying, for only so can the Lord Jesus be revealed constantly through us.[footnote3: 2 Cor. 4: 10.] All day long the choice will be before us in a thousand ways. It will mean no plans, no time, no money, no pleasure of our own. It will mean a constant yielding to those around us, for our yieldedness to God is measured by our yieldedness to man. Every humiliation, everyone who tries and vexes us, is God's way of breaking us, so that there is a yet deeper channel in us for the Life of Christ.

You see, the only life that pleases God and that can be victorious is His life-- never our life, no matter how hard we try. But inasmuch as our self-centred life is the exact opposite of His, we can never be filled with His life unless we are prepared for God to bring our life constantly to death. And in that we must co-operate by our moral choice.

CHAPTER 2.

CUPS RUNNING OVER

Brokenness, however, is but the beginning of Revival. Revival itself is being absolutely filled to overflowing with the Holy Spirit, and that is victorious living. If we were asked this moment if we were filled with the Holy Spirit, how many of us would dare to answer "yes"? Revival is when we can say "yes" at any moment of the day. It is not egoistic to say so, for filling to overflowing is utterly and completely God's work--it is all of grace. All we have to do is to present our empty, broken self and let Him fill and keep filled. Andrew Murray says, "Just as water ever seeks and fills the lowest place, so the moment God finds you abased and empty, His glory and power flow in." The picture that has made things simple and clear to so many of us is that of the human heart as a cup, which we hold out to Jesus, longing that He might fill it with the Water of Life. Jesus is pictured as bearing the golden water pot with the Water of Life. As He passes by, He looks into our cup and if it is clean, He fills to overflowing with the Water of Life. And as Jesus is always passing by, the cup can be always running over. That is something of what David meant, when he said, "My cup runneth over." This is Revival--you and I--full to overflowing with blessing ourselves and to others--with a constant peace in our hearts. People imagine that dying to self makes one miserable. But it just the opposite. It is the refusal to die to self that makes one miserable. The more we know of death with Him, the more we shall know of His life in us, and so the more of real peace and joy. His life, too, will overflow through us to lost souls in a real concern for their salvation, and to our fellow Christians in a deep desire for their blessing.

Under the Blood.

Only one thing prevents Jesus filling our cups as He passes by, and that is sin in one of its thousand forms. The Lord Jesus does not fill dirty cups. Anything that springs from self, however small it may be, is sin. Self-energy or self-complacency in service is sin. Self-pity in trials or difficulties, self-seeking in business or Christian work, self-indulgence in one's spare time, sensitiveness, touchiness, resentment and self-defence when we are hurt or injured by others, self-consciousness, reserve, worry, fear, all spring from self and all are sin and make our cups unclean.[*] But all of them were put into that other cup, which the Lord Jesus shrank from momentarily in Gethsemane, but which He drank to the dregs at Calvary--the cup of our sin. And if we will allow Him to show us what is in our cups and then give it to Him, He will cleanse them in the precious Blood that still flows for sin. That does not mean mere cleansing from the guilt of sin, nor even from the stain of sin--though thank God both of these are true--but from the sin itself, whatever it may be. And as He cleanses our cups, so He fills them to overflowing with His Holy Spirit.

And we are able daily to avail ourselves of that precious Blood. Suppose you have let the Lord Jesus cleanse your cup and have trusted Him to fill it to overflowing, then something comes along--a touch of envy or temper. What happens? Your cup becomes dirty and it ceases to overflow. And if we are constantly being defeated in this way, then our cup is never overflowing.

If we are to know continuous Revival, we must learn the way to keep our cups clean. It is never God's will that a Revival should cease, and be known in history as the Revival of this or that year. When that happens it is due to only one thing-- sin, just those little sins that the devil drops into our cup. But if we will go back to Calvary and learn afresh the power of the Blood of Jesus to cleanse moment by moment from the beginnings of sin, then we have learnt the secret of cups constantly cleansed and constantly overflowing. The moment you are conscious of that touch of envy, criticism, irritability, whatever it is--ask Jesus to cover it with His precious Blood and cleanse it away and you will find the reaction gone, your joy and peace restored and your cup running over. And the more you trust the Blood of Jesus in this way, the less will you even have these reactions. But cleansing is only possible when we have first been broken before God on the point concerned. Suppose we are irritated by certain traits in someone. It is not enough just to take our reactions of irritation to Calvary. We must first be broken, that is, we must yield to God over the whole question and accept that person and his ways as His will for us. Then we are able to take our wrong reaction to Jesus, knowing that His Blood will cleanse away our sin; and when we have been cleansed from sin, let us not keep mourning over it, let us not be occupied with ourselves. But let us look up to our victorious Lord, and praise Him that He is still victorious.

There is one simple but all-inclusive guide the Word of God gives to regulate our walk with Jesus and to make us to know when sin has come in. Colossians 3:15 says, "Let the peace of God rule in your hearts." Everything that disturbs the peace of God in our hearts is sin, no matter how small it is, and no matter how little like sin it may at first appear to be. This peace is to "rule" our hearts, or (a more literal translation) "be the referee" in our hearts. When the referee blows his whistle at a football match, the game has to stop, a foul has been committed. When we lose our peace, God's referee in our hearts has blown his whistle! Let us stop immediately, ask God to show us what is wrong, put by faith the sin He shows us under the Blood of Jesus, and then peace will be restored and we shall go on our way with our cups running over. If, however, God does not give us His peace, it will be because we are not really broken. Perhaps we have yet to say "sorry" to somebody else as well as to God. Or perhaps we still feel it is the other person's fault. But if we have lost our peace, it is obvious whose fault it is. We do not lose peace with God over another person's sin, but only over our own. God wants to show us our reactions, and only when we are willing to be cleansed there, will we have His peace. Oh, what a simple but searching thing it is to be ruled by the peace of God, none other than the Holy Spirit Himself! Former selfish ways, which we never bothered about, are now shown to us and we cannot walk in them without the referee blowing his whistle. Grumbling, bossiness, carelessness, down to the smallest thing are all revealed as sins, when we are prepared to let our days be ruled by the peace of God. Many times a day and over the smallest things we shall have to avail ourselves of the cleansing Blood of Jesus, and we shall find ourselves walking the way of brokenness as never before. But Jesus will be manifested in all His loveliness and grace in that brokenness.

Many of us, however, have neglected the referee's whistle so often and for so long that we have ceased to hear it. Days follow days and we feel we have little need of cleansing and no occasion of being broken. In that condition we are usually in a worse state than we ever imagine. It will need a great hunger for restored fellowship with God to possess our hearts before we will be willing to cry to God to show us where the Blood of Jesus must be applied. He will show us, to begin with, just one thing, and it will be our obedience and brokenness on that one thing that will be the first step into Revival for us.

[footnote*:Some may be inclined to question whether it is right to call such things as self-consciousness, reserve and fear, sins. "Call them infirmities, disabilities, temperamental weaknesses, if you will," some have said, "but not sins. To do so would be to get us into bondage." The reverse, however, is true. If these things are not sins, then we must put up with them for the rest of our lives, there is no deliverance. But if these and other things like them are indeed sins, then there is a Fountain for sin, and we may experience cleansing and deliverance from them, if we put them immediately under His precious Blood, the moment we are conscious of them. And they are sins. Their source is unbelief and an inverted form of pride, and they have hindered and hidden Him times without number.]

CHAPTER 3.

THE WAY OF FELLOWSHIP

When man fell and chose to make himself, rather than God, the centre of his life, the effect was not only to put man out of fellowship with God, but also out of fellowship with his fellow man. The story of man's first quarrel with God in the third chapter of Genesis is closely followed, in the fourth chapter, by the story of man's first quarrel with his fellow, Cain's murder of Abel. The Fall is simply, "we have turned every one to his own way."[footnote1: Is. 53: 6] If I want my own way rather than God's, it is quite obvious that I shall want my own way rather than the other man's. A man does not assert his independence of God to surrender it to a fellow man, if he can help it. But a world in which each man wants his own way cannot but be a world full of tensions, barriers, suspicions, misunderstandings, clashes and conflicts.

Now the work of the Lord Jesus Christ on the Cross was not only to bring men back into fellowship with God, but also into fellowship with their fellow men. Indeed it cannot do one without the other. As the spokes get nearer the centre of the wheel, they get nearer to one another. But if we have not been brought into vital fellowship with our brother, it is a proof that to that extent we have not been brought into vital fellowship with God. The first epistle of John (what a new light Revival sheds on this Scripture!) insists on testing the depth and reality of a man's fellowship with God by the depth and reality of his fellowship with his brethren.[footnote2:I John 2:9,3:14-15,4:20]

Some of us have come to see how utterly connected a man's relationship to his fellows is with his relationship to God. Everything that comes as a barrier between us and another, be it never so small, comes as a barrier between us and God. We have found that where these barriers are not put right immediately, they get thicker and thicker until we find ourselves shut off from God and our brother by what seem to be veritable brick walls. Quite obviously, if we allow New Life to come to us, it will have to manifest itself by a walk of oneness with God and our brother, with nothing between.

Light and Darkness.

On what basis can we have real fellowship with God and our brother? Here 1 John 1:7 has come afresh to us. "If we walk in the light, as He is in the light, we have fellowship one with another, and the Blood of Jesus Christ, His Son, cleanseth us from all sin." What is meant by light and darkness is that light reveals, darkness hides. When anything reproves us, shows us up as we really are--that is light.

"Whatsoever doth make manifest is light."[footnote3:Eph.5: 13] But whenever we do anything or say anything (or don't say anything) to hide what we are or what we've done--that is darkness.

Now the first effect of sin in our lives is always to make us try and hide what we are. Sin made our first parents hide behind the trees of the garden and it has had the same effect on us ever since. Sin always involves us in being unreal, pretending, duplicity, window dressing, excusing ourselves and blaming others--and we can do all that as much by our silence as by saying or doing something. This is what the previous verse calls "walking in darkness." With some of us, the sin in question may be nothing more than self-consciousness (anything with "I" in it is sin) and the hiding, nothing more than an assumed heartiness to cover that self-consciousness, but it is walking in darkness none the less.

In contrast to all this in us, verse 5 of this chapter tells us that "God is light," that is, God is the All-revealing One, who shows up every man as he really is. And it goes on to say, "In Him is no darkness at all," that is, there is absolutely nothing in God which can be one with the tiniest bit of darkness or hiding in us.

Quite obviously, then, it is utterly impossible for us to be walking in any degree of darkness and have fellowship with God. While we are in that condition of darkness, we cannot have true fellowship with our brother either--for we are not real with him, and no one can have fellowship with an unreal person. A wall of reserve separates him and us.

The Only Basis for Fellowship.

The only basis for real fellowship with God and man is to live out in the open with both. "But if we walk in the light, as He is in the light, we have fellowship one with another." To walk in the light is the opposite of walking in darkness. Spurgeon defines it in one of his sermons as "the willingness to know and be known." As far as God is concerned, this means that we are willing to know the whole truth about ourselves, we are open to conviction. We will bend the neck to the first twinges of conscience. Everything He shows us to be sin, we will deal with as sin--we will hide or excuse nothing. Such a walk in the light cannot but discover sin increasingly in our lives, and we shall see things to be sin which we never thought to be such before. For that reason we might shrink from this walk, and be tempted to make for cover. But the verse goes on with the precious words, "and the Blood of Jesus Christ, His Son, cleanseth us from all sin." Everything that the light of God shows up as sin, we can confess and carry to the Fountain of Blood and it is gone, gone from God's sight and gone from our hearts. By the power of the precious Blood we can be made more stainless than the driven snow; and thus continually abiding in the light and cleansed by the Blood, we have fellowship with God.

But the fellowship promised us here is not only with God, but "one with another"; and that involves us in walking in the light with our brother too. In any case, we cannot be "in the open" with God and "in the dark" with him. This means that we must be as willing to know the truth about ourselves from our brother as to know it from God. We must be prepared for him to hold the light to us (and we must be willing to do the same service for him) and challenge us in love about anything he sees in our lives which is not the highest. We must be willing not only to know, but to be known by him for what we really are. That means we are not going to hide our inner selves from those with whom we ought to be in fellowship; we are not going to window dress and put on appearances; nor are we going to whitewash and excuse ourselves. We are going to be honest about ourselves with them. We are willing to give up our spiritual privacy, pocket our pride and risk our reputations for the sake of being open and transparent with our brethren in Christ. It means, too, that we are not going to cherish any wrong feeling in our hearts about another, but we are first going to claim deliverance from it from God and put it right with the one concerned. As we walk this way, we shall find that we shall have fellowship with one another at an altogether new level, and we shall not love one another less, but infinitely more.

No Bondage.

Walking in the light is simply walking with Jesus. Therefore there need be no bondage about it. We have not necessarily got to tell everybody everything about ourselves. The fundamental thing is our attitude of walking in the light, rather than the act. Are we willing to be in the open with our brother--and be so in word when God tells us to? That is the "armour of light"--true transparency. This may sometimes be humbling, but it will help us to a new reality with Christ, and to a new self-knowledge. We have become so used to the fact that God knows all about us that it does not seem to register with us, and we inevitably end by not knowing the truth about ourselves. But let a man begin to be absolutely honest about himself with but one other, as God guides him, and he will come to a knowledge of himself and his sins that he never had before, and he will begin to see more clearly than ever before where the redemption of Christ has got to be applied progressively to his life. This is the reason why James tells us to put ourselves under the discipline of "confessing our faults one to another."

In 1 John 1:7, of course, the purpose of "walking in the light" is that we might "have fellowship one with another." And what fellowship it is when we walk this way together! Obviously, love will flow from one to another, when each is prepared to be known as the repentant sinner he is at the Cross of Jesus. When the barriers are down and the masks are off, God has a chance of making us really one. But there is also the added joy of knowing that in such a fellowship we are "safe." No fear now that others may be thinking thoughts about us or having reactions toward us, which they are hiding from us. In a fellowship which is committed to walk in the light beneath the Cross, we know that if there is any thought about us, it will quickly be brought into the light, either in brokenness and confession (where there has been wrong and unlove), or else as a loving challenge, as something that we ought to know about ourselves.

It must not, however, be forgotten that our walk in the light is first and foremost with the Lord Jesus. It is with Him first that we must get things settled and it is His cleansing and victory that must first be obtained. Then when God guides us to open our hearts with others, we come to them with far more of a testimony than a confession (except where that is specifically due) and we praise God together.

Teams of Two for Revival.

Jesus wants you to begin walking in the light with Him in a new way today. Join with one other--your Christian friend, the person you live with, your wife, your husband. Drop the mask. God has doubtless convicted you of one thing more than another that you have got to be honest with them about. Start there. Be a team of two to work for revival amongst your circle. As others are broken at the Cross they will be added to your fellowship, as God leads. Get together from time to time for fellowship and to share your spiritual experience with real openness. In complete oneness pray together for others, and go out as a team with fresh testimony. God through such a fellowship will begin to work wondrously. As He saves and blesses others in this vital way, they can start to live and work as a fellowship too. As one billiard ball will move another billiard ball, so one group will set off another group, until the whole of our land is covered with New Life from the risen Lord Jesus.

CHAPTER 4.

THE HIGHWAY OF HOLINESS

One of the things that we must learn if we are to live the victorious Christian life is its utter simplicity. How complicated we have made it! Great volumes are written, all sorts of technical phrases are used, we are told the secret lies in this, or that and so on. But to most of us, it is all so complicated that, although we know it in theory, we are unable to relate what we know to our practical daily living. In order to make the simple truths we have been considering even clearer, we want in this chapter to cast them all in picture form.

The Highway.

An "over-all" picture of the life of victory, which has come to many of us is that of the Highway in Isaiah 35: "And an highway shall be there and a way and it shall be called the way of holiness." The picture is that of a Highway built up from the surrounding morass, the world. Though the Highway is narrow and uphill, it is not beyond any of us to walk it, for "the wayfaring men, though fools, shall not err therein." Though there are many dangers if we get off the road, while we keep to the Highway there is safety, for "no lion shall be there, nor any ravenous beast shall go up thereon." Only one kind of person is barred from walking there and that is the unclean one. "The unclean shall not pass over it." This includes not only the sinner who does not know Christ as his Saviour, but the Christian who does and yet is walking in unconfessed and uncleansed sin.

The only way on to the Highway is up a small dark, forbidding hill--the Hill of Calvary. It is the sort of hill we have to climb on our hands and knees--especially our knees. If we are content with our present Christian life, if we do not desire with a desperate hunger to get on to the Highway, we shall never get to our knees and thus never climb the hill. But if we are dissatisfied, if we are hungry, then we will find ourselves ascending. Don't hurry. Let God make you really hungry for the Highway; let Him really drive you to your knees in longing prayer. Mere sightseers won't get very far. "Ye shall find Me when ye shall search for Me with all your heart."

A Low Door.

At the top of the hill, guarding the way to the Highway, stands so gaunt and grim ... the Cross. There it stands, the Divider of time and the Divider of men. At the foot of the Cross is a low door, so low that to get through it one has to stoop and crawl through. It is the only entrance to the Highway. We must go through it if we would go any further on our way. This door is called the Door of the Broken Ones. Only the broken can enter the Highway. To be broken means to be "not I, but Christ." There is in every one of us a proud, stiff-necked "I." The stiff neck began in the Garden of Eden when Adam and Eve, who had always bowed their heads in surrender to God's will, stiffened their necks, struck out for independence and tried to be "as gods." All the way through the Bible, God charges His people with the same stiff neck; and it manifests itself in us, too. We are hard and unyielding. We are sensitive and easily hurt. We get irritable, envious and critical. We are resentful and unforgiving. We are self-indulgent--and how often that can lead to impurity! Every one of these things, and many more, spring from this proud self within. If it were not there and Christ were in its place, we would not have these reactions. Before we can enter the Highway, God must bend and break that stiff-necked self, so that Christ reigns in its stead. To be broken means to have no rights before God and man. It does not mean merely surrendering my rights to Him but rather recognising that I haven't any, except to deserve hell. It means just being nothing and having nothing that I call my own, neither time, money, possessions nor position.

In order to break our wills to His, God brings us to the foot of the Cross and there shows us what real brokenness is. We see those wounded Hands and Feet, that Face of Love crowned with thorns and we see the complete brokenness of the One who said, "Not my will, but Thine be done," as He drank the bitter cup of our sin to its dregs. So the way to be broken is to look on Him and to realise it was our sin which nailed Him there. Then as we see the love and brokenness of the God who died in our place, our hearts will become strangely melted and we will want to be broken for Him and we shall pray,

"Oh, to be saved from myself, dear Lord,

Oh, to be lost in Thee,

Oh, that it might be no more I,

But Christ that lives in me."

And some of us have found that there is no prayer that God is so swift to answer as the prayer that He might break us.

A Constant Choice.

But do not let us imagine that we have to be broken only once as we go through the door. Ever after it will be a constant choice before us. God brings His pressure to bear on us, but we have to make the choice. If someone hurts and slights us, we immediately have the choice of accepting the slight as a means of grace to humble us lower or we can resist it and stiffen our necks again with all the disturbance of

12

spirit that that is bound to bring. Right the way through the day our brokenness will be tested and it is no use our pretending we are broken before God, if we are not broken in our attitude to those around us. God nearly always tests us through other people. There are no second causes for the Christian. God's will is made known in His providence, and His providences are so often others with their many demands on us. If you find yourself in a patch of unbrokenness, the only way is to go afresh to Calvary and see Christ broken for you and you will come away willing to be broken for Him.

Over the Door of the Broken Ones is sprinkled the precious Blood of the Lord Jesus. As we bend to crawl through, the Blood cleanses from all sin. For not only have we to bend to get through, but only the clean can walk the Highway. Maybe you have never known Jesus as your Saviour, maybe you have known Him for years, but in either case you are defiled by sin, the sins of pride, envy, resentment, impurity, etc. If you will give them all to Him who bore them on the Cross, He will whisper to you again what He once said on the Cross, "It is finished," and your heart will be cleansed whiter than snow.

The Gift of His Fulness.

So we get on to the Highway. There it stretches before us, a narrow uphill road, bathed in light, leading towards the Heavenly Jerusalem. The embankment on either side slopes away into thick darkness. In fact, the darkness creeps right to the very edges of the Highway, but on the Highway itself all is light. Behind us is the Cross, no longer dark and forbidding, but radiant and glowing, and we no longer see Jesus stretched across its arms, but walking the Highway overflowing with resurrection life. In His Hands He carries a pitcher with the Water of Life. He comes right up to us and asks us to hold out our hearts, and just as if we were handing Him a cup, we present to Him our empty hearts. He looks inside--a painful scrutiny--and where He sees we have allowed His Blood to cleanse them, He fills them with the Water of Life. So we go on our way rejoicing and praising God and overflowing with His new life. This is revival. You and I full of the Holy Spirit all the time, loving others and concerned for their salvation. No struggling, no tarrying. Just simply giving Him each sin to cleanse in His precious Blood and accepting from His hands the free gift of His Fulness, and then allowing Him to do the work through us. As we walk along with Him, He is always there continually filling so that our cups continually overflow.

So the rest of our Christian life simply consists now of walking along the Highway, with hearts overflowing, bowing the neck to His will all the time, constantly trusting the Blood to cleanse us and living in complete oneness with Jesus. There is nothing spectacular about this life, no emotional experiences to sigh after and wait for. It is just plain day to day living the life the Lord intended us to live. This is real holiness.

Off the Highway.

But we may, and sometimes do, slip off the Highway, for it is narrow. One little step aside and we are off the path and in darkness. It is always because of a failure in obedience somewhere or a failure to be weak enough to let God do all. Satan is always beside the road, shouting at us, but he cannot touch us. But we can yield to his voice by an act of will. This is the beginning of sin and slipping away from Jesus. Sometimes we find ourselves stiffening our necks to someone, sometimes to God Himself. Sometimes jealousy or resentment assails us. Immediately we are over the side, for nothing unclean can walk the Highway. Our cup is dirtied and ceases to overflow and we lose our peace with God. If we do not come back to the Highway at once, we shall go further down the side. We must get back. How? The first thing to do is to ask God to show what caused us to slip off; and He will, though it often takes Him time to make us see. Perhaps someone annoyed me, and I was irritated. God wants me to see that it was not the thing that the person did that matters, but my reaction to it. If I had been broken, I would not have been irritated. So, as I look longingly back to the Highway, I see the Lord Jesus again and I see what an ugly thing it is to get irritable and that Jesus died to save me from being irritable. As I crawl up again to the Highway on hands and knees, I come again to Him and His Blood for cleansing. Jesus is waiting there to fill my cup to overflowing once again. Hallelujah! No matter where you leave the Highway, you will always find Him calling you to come back and be broken again, and always the Blood will be there to cleanse and make you clean. This is the great secret of the Highway--knowing what to do with sin, when sin has come in. The secret is always to take sin to the Cross, see there its sinfulness, and then put it under the Blood and reckon it gone.

So the real test all along the Highway will be--are our cups running over? Have we the peace of God in our hearts? Have we love and concern for others? These things are the barometer of the Highway. If they are disturbed, then sin has crept in somewhere--self-pity, self-seeking, self-indulgence in thought or deed, sensitiveness, touchiness, self-defence, self-consciousness, shyness, reserve, worry, fear and so on.

Our walk with Others.

An important thing about the Highway which has not been mentioned yet is that we do not walk this Highway alone. Others walk it with us. There is, of course, the Lord Jesus. But there are other wayfarers, too, and the rule of the road is that fellowship with them is as important as fellowship with Jesus. Indeed, the two are intimately connected. Our relationship with our fellows and our relationship with God are so linked that we cannot disturb one without disturbing the other. Everything that comes between us and another, such as impatience, resentment or envy, comes between us and God. These barriers are sometimes no more than veils--veils through which we can still, to some extent, see. But if not removed immediately, they thicken into blankets and then into brick walls, and we are shut off from both God and our fellows, shut in to ourselves. It is clear why these two relationships should be so linked. "God is love," that is love for others, and the moment we fail in love towards another, we put ourselves out of fellowship with God--for God loves him, even if we don't.

But more than that, the effect of such sins is always to make us "walk in darkness"--that is, to cover it up and hide what we really are or what we are really feeling. That is always the meaning of "darkness" in Scripture, for while the light reveals, the darkness hides. The first effect of sin in us is always to make us hide; with the result that we are pretending, we are wearing a mask, we are not real with either God or man. And, of course, neither God nor man can fellowship with an unreal person.

The way back into fellowship with the Lord Jesus will bring us again into fellowship with our brother, too. All unlove must be recognised as sin and given to the Lord Jesus for His Blood to cover--and then it can be put right with our brother also. As we come back to the Lord Jesus like this, we shall find His love for our brother filling our hearts and wanting to express itself in our actions toward him and we shall walk in fellowship together again.

So this is the Highway life. It is no new astounding doctrine. It is not something new for us to preach. It is quite unspectacular. It is just a life to live day by day in whatever circumstances the Lord has put us. It does not contradict what we may have read or heard about the Christian life. It just puts into simple pictorial language the great truths of sanctification. To start to live this life now will mean revival in our lives. To continue to live it will be revival continued. Revival is just you and I walking along the Highway in complete oneness with the Lord Jesus and with one another, with cups continually cleansed and overflowing with the life and love of God.

CHAPTER 5.

THE DOVE AND THE LAMB

Victorious living and effective soul-winning service are not the product of our better selves and hard endeavours, but are simply the fruit of the Holy Spirit. We are not called upon to produce the fruit, but simply to bear it. It is all the time to be His fruit. Nothing is more important then, than that we should be continuously filled with the Holy Spirit, or to keep to the metaphor, that the "trees of the Lord should be continuously full of sap"--His sap.

How this may be so for us is graphically illustrated by the record, in the first chapter of John, of how the Holy Spirit came upon the Lord Jesus at His baptism. John the Baptist had seen Jesus coming to Him and had said of Him, "Behold, the Lamb of God that beareth the sin of the world." Then as he baptised him, he saw the heavens opened and the Spirit of God descending like a Dove and lighting upon Him.

The Humility of God.

What a suggestive picture we have here--the Dove descending upon the Lamb and resting herself upon Him! The Lamb and the Dove are surely the gentlest of all God's creatures. The Lamb speaks of meekness and submissiveness and the Dove speaks of peace (what more peaceful sound than the cooing of a dove on a summer day). Surely this shows us that the heart of Deity is humility. When the eternal God chose to reveal Himself in His Son, He gave Him the name of the Lamb; and when it was necessary for the Holy Spirit to come into the world, He was revealed under the emblem of the Dove. Is it not obvious, then, that the reason why we have to be humble in order to walk with God is not merely because God is so big and we so little, that humility befits such little creatures--but because God is so humble?

The main lesson of this incident is that the Holy Spirit, as the Dove, could only come upon and remain upon the Lord Jesus because He was the Lamb. Had the Lord Jesus had any other disposition than that of the Lamb--humility, submissiveness and self-surrender--the Dove could never have rested on Him. Being herself so gentle, she would have been frightened away had not Jesus been meek and lowly in heart.

Here, then, we have pictured for us the condition upon which the same Holy Spirit can come upon us and abide upon us. The Dove can only abide upon us as we are willing to be as the Lamb. How impossible that He should rest upon us while self is unbroken! The manifestations of the unbroken self are the direct opposite of the gentleness of the Dove. Read again in Galatians 5 the ninefold fruit of the Spirit ("love, joy, peace, long-suffering, gentleness, goodness, faithfulness, meekness, self-control") with which the Dove longs to fill us! Then contrast it with the ugly works of the flesh (the N.T. name for the unbroken self) in the same chapter. It is the contrast of the snarling wolf with the gentle dove!

The Disposition of the Lamb.

How clear, then, that the Holy Spirit will only come upon us and remain upon us as we are willing to be as the Lamb on each point on which He will convict us! And nothing is so searching and humbling as to look at the Lamb on His way to Calvary for us and to be shown in how many points we have been unwilling to take the position of the lamb for Him.

Look at Him for a moment as the Lamb. He was the simple Lamb. A lamb is the simplest of God's creatures. It has no schemes or plans for helping itself--it exists in helplessness and simplicity. Jesus made Himself as nothing for us, and became the simple Lamb. He had no strength of His own or wisdom of His own, no schemes to get Himself out of difficulties, just simple dependence on the Father all the time. "The Son can do nothing of Himself, but what He seeth the Father do." But we-- how complicated we are! What schemes we have had of helping ourselves and of getting ourselves out of difficulties. What efforts of our own we have resorted to, to live the Christian life and to do God's works, as if we were something and could do something. The Dove had to take His flight (at least as far as the conscious blessing of His Presence was concerned) because we were not willing to be simple lambs.

Willing to be Shorn.

Then He was the shorn Lamb, willing to be shorn of His rights, His reputation, and every human liberty that was due to Him, just as a lamb is shorn of its wool. He never resisted: A lamb never does. When He was reviled for our sakes, He reviled not again. When He suffered, He threatened not. He never said, "You cannot treat me like that. Don't you know that I am the Son of God?" But we--ah we, on how many occasions have we been unwilling to be shorn of that which was our right. We were not willing for His sake to lose what was our own. We insisted, too, that we should be treated with the respect due to our position. We resisted, and we fought. The Dove had to take His flight from us for we were not willing to be shorn lambs, and we were left without peace, hard and unloving.

He Answered Nothing.

Then further, He was the silent Lamb. "As a sheep before her shearers is dumb, so He openeth not His mouth." Facing the calumnies of men, we read, "He answered nothing." He never defended Himself, nor explained Himself. But we have been anything but silent when others have said unkind or untrue things about us. Our voices have been loud in self-defence and self-vindication, and there has been anger in our voices. We have excused ourselves, when we should have admitted frankly our wrong. On every such occasion the Dove had to take His flight, and withdraw His peace and blessing from our hearts, because we were not willing to be the silent lamb.

No Grudges.

He was also the spotless Lamb. Not only did nothing escape His lips, but there was nothing in His heart but love for those who had sent Him to the Cross. There was no resentment towards them, no grudges, no bitterness. Even as they were putting the nails through His hands, He was murmuring, "I forgive you," and He asked His Father to forgive them too. He was willing to suffer it in meekness for us. But what resentment and bitterness have not we had in our hearts--toward this one and that one, and over so much less than what they did to Jesus. Each reaction left a stain on our hearts, and the Dove had to fly away because we were not willing to bear it and forgive it for Jesus' sake.

Return, O Dove!

These, then, are the acts and attitudes which drive the Holy Spirit from our lives, as far as present blessing is concerned, and they are all sin. Sin is the only thing that hinders the revival of His Church. The question of all questions for us just now is, "How can the Dove return to our lives with His peace and power?" The answer is again just simply, "The Lamb of God," for He is not only the simple Lamb and the shorn Lamb and the silent Lamb and the spotless Lamb, but above everything else He is the substitute Lamb.

To the Jew the lamb that was offered to God was always a substitute lamb. Its meekness and submissiveness was only incidental to its main work, that of being slain for his sin and of its blood being sprinkled on the altar to atone for it. The humility of the Lord Jesus in becoming our Lamb was necessary only that He might become on the Cross our Substitute, our scapegoat, carrying our sins in His own Body on the Tree, so that there might be forgiveness for our sins and cleansing from all their stains, when we repent of them. But inasmuch as there is no past or future with God, but all is present and timeless, there is a sense in which the suffering of the Lord Jesus for the sins of which we have not repented is present too. What a vision it is when we see these sins wounding and hurting Him now! May this solemn thought break our proud hearts in repentance! For it is only when we have seen these sins of ours in the heart of Jesus, so that we are broken and willing to repent of them and put them right, that the Blood of the Lamb cleanses us from them and the Dove returns with peace and blessing to our hearts.

He humbled Himself to the manger,

And even to Calvary's tree;

But I am so proud and unwilling,

His humble disciple to be.

He yielded His will to the Father,

And chose to abide in the Light;

But I prefer wrestling to resting,

And try by myself to do right.

Lord break me, then cleanse me and fill me

And keep me abiding in Thee;

That fellowship may be unbroken,

And Thy Name be hallowed in me.

A saintly African Christian told a congregation once that, as he was climbing the hill to the meeting, he heard steps behind him. He turned and saw a man carrying a very heavy load up the hill on his back. He was full of sympathy for him and spoke to him. Then he noticed that His hands were scarred, and he realised that it was Jesus. He said to Him, "Lord, are you carrying the world's sins up the hill?" "No," said the Lord Jesus, "not the world's sin, just yours!" As that African simply told the vision God had just given him, the people's hearts and his heart were broken as they saw their sins at the Cross. Our hearts need to be broken too, and only when they are, shall we be willing for the confessions, the apologies, the reconciliations and the restitutions, that are involved in a true repentance of sin. Then, when we have been willing to humble ourselves, as the Lord humbled Himself, the Dove will return to us.

Return, O heavenly Dove, return,

Sweet messenger of rest!

I hate the sins that made Thee mourn,

And drove Thee from my breast.

Ruled by the Dove.

One last word. The Dove is the emblem of peace, which suggests that if the Blood of Jesus has cleansed us and we are walking with the Lamb in humility, the sign of the Spirit's presence and fulness will be peace. This is indeed to be the test of our walk all the way along. "Let the peace of God rule (or arbitrate) in your hearts" (Col. 3:15). If the Dove ceases to sing in our hearts at any time, if our peace is broken, then it can only be because of sin. In some matter we have departed from the humility of the Lamb. We must ask God to show us what it is, and be quick to repent of it and bring the sin to the Cross. Then the Dove will be once again in His rightful place in our hearts and peace with God will be ours. In this way we shall know that continuous abiding of the Spirit's presence, which is open even to fallen men through the immediate and constant application of the precious Blood of Jesus.

Shall we not begin from today to allow our lives to be ruled by the Heavenly Dove, the peace of God, and allow Him to be the arbiter all the day through? We shall find ourselves walking in a path of constant conviction and much humbling, but in this way we shall come into real conformity with the Lamb of God, and we shall know the only victory that is worth anything, the conquest of self.

CHAPTER 6.

REVIVAL IN THE HOME

Thousands of years ago, in the most beautiful Garden the world has ever known, lived a man and a woman. Formed in the likeness of their Creator, they lived solely to reveal Him to His creation and to each other and thus to glorify Him every moment of the day. Humbly they accepted the position of a creature with the Creator--that of complete submission and yieldedness to His will. Because they always submitted their wills to His, because they lived for Him and not for themselves, they were also completely submitted to each other. Thus in that first home in that beautiful garden, there was absolute harmony, peace, love and oneness not only with God, but with each other.

Then one day, the harmony was shattered, for the serpent stole into that God-centred home, and with him, sin. And now, because they had lost their peace and fellowship with God, they lost it with each other. No longer did they live for God--they each lived for themselves. They were each their own gods now, and because they no longer lived for God, they no longer lived for each other. Instead of peace, harmony, love and oneness--there was now discord and hate--in other words, SIN!

Revival begins in the Home.

It was into the home that sin first came. It is in the home that we sin more than perhaps anywhere else, and it is to the home that revival first needs to come. Revival is desperately needed in the church--in the country--in the world, but a revived church with unrevived homes would be sheer hypocrisy. It is the hardest place, the most costly, but the most necessary place to begin.

But before we go on, let us remind ourselves again of what revival really is. It simply means new life, in hearts where the spiritual life has ebbed--but not a new life of self-effort or self-initiated activity. It is not man's life, but God's life, the life of Jesus filling us and flowing through us. That Life is manifested in fellowship and oneness with those with whom we live--nothing between us and God, and nothing between us and others. The home is the place before all others where this should be experienced.

But how different is the experience of so many of us professing Christians in our homes--little irritations, frayed tempers, selfishness and resentments; and even where there is nothing very definitely wrong between us, just not that complete oneness and fellowship that ought to characterise Christians living together. All the things that come between us and others, come between us and God and spoil our fellowship with Him, so that our hearts are not overflowing with the Divine Life.

What is wrong with our Homes?

Now what at bottom is wrong with our homes? When we talk about homes, we mean the relationship which exists between a husband and wife, a parent and child, a brother and sister, or between any others who, through various circumstances are compelled to live together.

The first thing that is wrong with so many families is that they are not really open with one another. We live so largely behind drawn blinds. The others do not know us for what we really are, and we do not intend that they should. Even those living in the most intimate relationships with us do not know what goes on inside-- our difficulties, battles, failures, nor what the Lord Jesus has to cleanse us from so frequently. This lack of transparency and openness is ever the result of sin. The first effect of the first sin was to make Adam and Eve hide from God behind the trees of the Garden. They who had been so transparent with God and with one another were then hiding from God, because of sin; and if they hid from God you can be quite sure that they soon began to hide from one another. There were reactions and thoughts in Adam's heart that Eve was never allowed to know and there were like things hidden in Eve's heart too. And so it has been ever since. Having something to hide from God, we hide it, too, from one another. Behind that wall of reserve, which acts like a mask, we cover our real selves. Sometimes we hide in the most extraordinary way behind an assumed jocular manner. We are afraid to be serious because we do not want others to get too close and see us as we really are, and so we keep up a game of bluff. We are not real with one another, and no one can have fellowship with an unreal person, and so oneness and close fellowship are impossible in the home. This is what the Scripture calls "walking in darkness"--for the darkness is anything which hides.

The Failure to Love.

The second thing that is wrong with our homes is our failure really to love one another. "Well," says somebody, "that could never be said of our home, for no one could love one another more than my husband and I love each other!" But wait a minute! It depends on what you mean by love. Love is not just a sentimental feeling, nor even strong passion. The famous passage in 1 Corinthians 13 tells us what real love is, and if we test ourselves by it, we may find that after all we are hardly loving one another at all, and our behaviour is all in the opposite direction--and the opposite of love is hate! Let us look at some of the things that that passage tells us about love.

"Love is long suffering (patient) and is kind."

"Love vaunteth not itself (does not boast) is not puffed up (is not conceited)."

"Love does not behave itself unseemly (is not rude) seeketh not her own (is not selfish), is not easily provoked (does not get irritated), thinketh no evil (does not entertain unkind thoughts of another)."

How do we stand up to those tests in our homes? So often we act in the very opposite way.

We are often impatient with one another and even unkind in the way we answer back or react.

How much envy, too, there can be in a home. A husband and wife can envy the other their gifts, even their spiritual progress. Parents may be envious of their children, and how often is there not bitter envy between brothers and sisters.

Also "not behaving unseemly," that is, courtesy, what about that? Courtesy is just love in little things, but it is in the little things that we trip up. We think we can "let up" at home.

How "puffed up," that is, conceited, we so often are! Conceit comes out in all sorts of ways. We think we know best, we want our way and we nag or boss the other one; and nagging or bossing leads on to the tendency to despise the other one. Our very attitude of superiority sets us up above them. Then, when at the bottom of our hearts we despise someone, we blame them for everything--and yet we think we love.

Then what about "seeking not our own," that is, not being selfish? Many times a day we put our wishes and interests before those of the other one.

How "easily provoked" we are! How quick to be irritated by something in the other. How often we allow the unkind thought, the resentful feeling over something the other has done or left undone! Yet we profess there are no failures in love in our homes. These things happen every day and we think nothing of them. They are all of them the opposite of love, and the opposite of love is hate. Impatience is hate, envy is hate, conceit and self-will are hate, and so are selfishness, irritability and resentment! And hate is SIN. "He that saith he is in the light and hateth his brother, is in the darkness even until now." What tensions, barriers and discord it all causes, and fellowship with both God and the other is made impossible.

The Only Way Out.

Now the question is, do I want new life, revival, in my home? I have got to challenge my heart about this. Am I prepared to continue in this state or am I really hungry for new life, His life, in my home? For not unless I am really hungry will I be willing to take the necessary steps. The first step I must take is to call sin, sin (my sin, not the other person's) and go with it to the Cross, and trust the Lord Jesus there and then to cleanse me from it.

As we bow the neck at the Cross, His self-forgetful love for the others, His longsuffering and forbearance flow into our hearts. The precious Blood cleanses us from the unlove and ill will and the Holy Spirit fills us with the very nature of Jesus. 1 Corinthians 13 is nothing less than the nature of Jesus, and it is all gift to us, for His nature is ours, if He is ours. This blessed process can happen every single time the beginnings of sin and unlove creep in, for the cleansing fountain of Blood is available to us all the time.

All this will commit us very definitely to walking the Way of the Cross in our homes. Again and again we will see places where we must yield up our rights, as Jesus yielded up His for us. We shall have to see that the thing in us that reacts so sharply to another's selfishness and pride, is simply our own selfishness and pride, which we are unwilling to sacrifice. We shall have to accept another's ways and doings as God's will for us and meekly bend the neck to all God's providences. That does not mean that we must accept another's selfishness as God's will for them-- far from it--but only as God's will for us. As far as the other is concerned, God will probably want to use us, if we are broken, to help him see his need. Certainly, if we are a parent we shall often need to correct our child with firmness. But none of this is to be from selfish motives, but only out of love for the other and a longing for their good. Our own convenience and rights must all the time be yielded. Only so will the love of the Lord Jesus be able to fill us and express itself through us.

When we have been broken at Calvary, we must be willing to put things right with the others--sometimes even with the children. This is, so often, the test of our brokenness. Brokenness is the opposite of hardness. Hardness says, "It's your fault!" Brokenness, however, says, "It's my fault!" What a different atmosphere will begin to prevail in our homes when they hear us say that. Let us remember that at the Cross there is only room for one at a time. We cannot say, "I was wrong, but you were wrong too. You must come as well!" No, you must go alone, saying, "I'm wrong." God will work in the other more through your brokenness than through anything else you can do or say. We may, however, have to wait--perhaps a long time. But that should only give us to feel more with God, for, as someone has said, "He too has had to wait a long time since His great attempt to put things right with man nineteen hundred years ago, although there was no wrong on His side." But God will surely answer our prayer and bring the other to Calvary too. There we shall be one; there the middle wall of partition between us will be broken down; there we shall be able to walk in the light, in true transparency, with Jesus and with one another, loving each other with a pure heart fervently. Sin is almost the only thing we have in common with everyone else, and so at the feet of Jesus where sin is cleansed is the only place where we can be one. Real oneness conjures up for us the picture of two or more sinners together at Calvary.

CHAPTER 7.

THE MOTE AND THE BEAM

That friend of ours has got something in his eye! Though it is only something tiny--what Jesus called a mote--how painful it is and how helpless he is until it is removed! It is surely our part as a friend to do all we can to remove it, and how grateful he is to us when we have succeeded in doing so. We should be equally grateful to him, if he did the same service for us.

In the light of that, it seems clear that the real point of the well-known passage in Matthew 7:3-5 about the beam and the mote is not the forbidding of our trying to remove the fault in the other person, but rather the reverse. It is the injunction that at all costs we should do this service for one another. True, its first emphasis seems to be a condemnation of censoriousness, but when the censoriousness in us is removed, the passage ends by saying, "Then shalt thou see clearly to cast the mote out of thy brother's eye." According to the New Testament, we are meant to care so much for the other man, that we are willing to do all we can to remove from his eye the mote which is marring his vision and hindering his blessing. We are told to "admonish one another" and "exhort one another" and to "wash one another's feet" and "to provoke one another to love and good works." The love of Jesus poured out in us will make us want to help our brother in this way.

What blessing may not come to many others through our willingness humbly to challenge one another, as led by God. A humble Swiss, named Nicholas of Basle, one of the Society of the "Friends of God," crossed the mountains to Strassbourg and entered the Church of Dr. Tauler, the popular preacher of that city. Said Nicholas, "Dr. Tauler, before you can do your greatest work for God, the world and this city, you must die--die to yourself, your gifts, your popularity, and even your own goodness, and when you have learned the full meaning of the Cross, you will have a new power with God and man." That humble challenge from an obscure Christian changed Dr. Tauler's life, and he did indeed learn to die, and became one of the great factors to prepare the way for Luther and the Reformation. In this passage the Lord Jesus tells us how we may do this service for one another.

What is the Beam?

First, however, the Lord Jesus tells us that it is only too possible to try to take the tiny mote, a tiny speck of sawdust, out of the other's eye when there is a beam, a great length of timber, in ours. When that is the case, we haven't a chance of casting out the mote in the other, because we cannot see straight ourselves, and in any case it is sheer hypocrisy to attempt to do so.

Now we all know what Jesus meant by the mote in the other person's eye. It is some fault which we fancy we can discern in him; it may be an act he has done against us, or some attitude he adopts towards us. But what did the Lord Jesus mean by the beam in our eye? I suggest that the beam in our eye is simply our unloving reaction to the other man's mote. Without doubt there is a wrong in the other person. But our reaction to that wrong is wrong too! The mote in him has provoked in us resentment, or coldness, or criticism, or bitterness, or evil speaking, or ill will--all of them variants of the basic ill, unlove. And that, says the Lord Jesus, is far, far worse than the tiny wrong (sometimes quite unconscious) that provoked it. A mote means in the Greek a little splinter, whereas a beam means a rafter. And the Lord Jesus means by this comparison to tell us that our unloving reaction to the other's wrong is what a great rafter is to a little splinter! Every time we point one of our fingers at another and say, "It's your fault," three of our fingers are pointing back at us. God have mercy on us for the many times when it has been so with us and when in our hypocrisy we have tried to deal with the person's fault, when God saw there was this thing far worse in our own hearts.

But let us not think that a beam is of necessity some violent reaction on our part. The first beginning of a resentment is a beam, as is also the first flicker of an unkind thought, or the first suggestion of unloving criticism. Where that is so, it only distorts our vision and we shall never see our brother as he really is, beloved of God. If we speak to our brother with that in our hearts, it will only provoke him to adopt the same hard attitude to us, for it is a law of human relationships that "with what measure ye mete, it shall be measured to you again."

Take it to Calvary.

No! "First cast out the beam out of thine own eye." That is the first thing we must do. We must recognise our unloving reaction to him as sin. On our knees we must go with it to Calvary and see Jesus there and get a glimpse of what that sin cost Him. At His Feet we must repent of it and be broken afresh and trust the Lord Jesus to cleanse it away in His precious Blood and fill us with His love for that one--and He will, and does, if we will claim His promise. Then we shall probably need to go to the other in the attitude of the repentant one, tell him of the sin that has been in our heart and what the Blood has effected there and ask him to forgive us too. Very often bystanders will tell us, and sometimes our own hearts, that the sin we are confessing is not nearly so bad as the other's wrong, which he is not yet confessing. But we have been to Calvary, indeed we are learning to live under the shadow of Calvary, and we have seen our sin there and we can no longer compare our sin with another's. But as we take these simple steps of repentance, then we see clearly to cast out the mote out of the other's eye, for the beam in our eye has gone. In that moment God will pour light in on us as to the other's need, that neither he nor we ever had before. We may see then that the mote we were so conscious of before, is virtually non-existent--it was but the projection of something that was in us. On the other hand, we may have revealed to us hidden underlying things, of which he himself was hardly conscious.

Then as God leads us, we must lovingly and humbly challenge him, so that he may see them too, and bring them to the Fountain for sin and find deliverance. He will be more likely than ever to let us do it--indeed if he is a humble man, he will be grateful to us, for he will know now that there is no selfish motive in our heart, but only love and concern for him.

When God is leading us to challenge another, let not fear hold us back. Let us not argue or press our point. Let us just say what God has told us to and leave it there. It is God's work, not ours, to cause the other to see it. It takes time to be willing to bend "the proud stiff-necked I." When we in turn are challenged, let us not defend ourselves and explain ourselves. Let us take it in silence, thanking the other; and then go to God about it and ask Him. If he was right, let us be humble enough to go and tell him, and praise God together. There is no doubt that we need each other desperately. There are blind spots in all our lives that we shall never see, unless we are prepared for another to be God's channel to us.

CHAPTER 8.

ARE YOU WILLING TO BE A SERVANT?

Nothing is clearer from the New Testament than that the Lord Jesus expects us to take the low position of servants. This is not just an extra obligation, which we may or may not assume as we please. It is the very heart of that new relationship which the disciple is to take up to God and to his fellows if he is to know fellowship with Christ and any degree of holiness in his life. When we understand the humbling and self-emptying that is involved in really being a servant, it becomes evident that only those who are prepared to live quite definitely under the shadow of Calvary, ever contemplating the humility and brokenness of the Lord Jesus for us, will be willing for that position.

As we approach this subject and its personal application in detail to our lives, there are three preliminary things which need to be said to prepare us to understand the low and humbling position which He wants us to take.

In the Old Testament two sorts of servants are mentioned. There are the hired servants, who have wages paid to them and have certain rights. Then there are the bond-servants, or slaves, who have no rights, who receive no wages and who have no appeal. The Hebrews were forbidden ever to make bond-servants of their own race. Only of the Gentiles were they permitted to take such slaves. When, however, we come to the New Testament, the word in the Greek for the servant of the Lord Jesus Christ is not "hired servant" but "bond-servant," by which is meant to be shown that our position is one where we have no rights and no appeal, where we are the absolute property of our Master, to be treated and disposed of just as He wishes.

Further, we shall see more clearly still what our position is to be when we understand that we are to be the bond-servants of One who was Himself willing to be a bond-servant. Nothing shows better the amazing humility of the Lord Jesus, whose servants we are to be, than that "though He was in the form of God, He counted it not a prize to be on an equality with God, but emptied Himself and took upon Him the form of a bondservant" (Phil. 2:6,7)--without rights, willing to be treated as the will of the Father and the malice of men might decree, if only He might thereby serve men and bring them back to God. And you and I are to be the bond-servants of Him who was and always is a bondservant, whose disposition is ever that of humility and whose activity is ever that of humbling Himself to serve His creatures. How utterly low, then, is our true position! How this shows us what it means to be ruled by the Lord Jesus!

That leads us to something further. Our servanthood to the Lord Jesus is to express itself in our servanthood to our fellows. Says Paul, "We preach not ourselves, but Christ Jesus, the Lord, and ourselves your bond-servants for Jesus' sake." The low position we take toward the Lord Jesus is judged by Him by the low position we take in our relationship with our fellows. An unwillingness to serve others in costly, humbling ways He takes to be an unwillingness to serve Him, and we thus put ourselves out of fellowship with Him.

We are now in a position to apply all this much more personally to our lives. God spoke to me some time ago through Luke 17:7-1O. "But which of you, having a servant plowing or feeding cattle, will say unto him by and by, when he is come from the field, Go and sit down to meat? And will not rather say unto him, Make ready wherewith I may sup, and gird thyself and serve me, till I have eaten and drunken; and afterwards thou shalt eat and drink? Doth he thank that servant because he did the things that were commanded him? I trow not. So likewise ye, when ye shall have done all those things which are commanded you, say, We are unprofitable servants; we have done that which was our duty to do."

I see here five marks of the bond-servant. First of all, he must be willing to have one thing on top of another put upon him, without any consideration being given him. On top of a hard day in the field the servant in the parable had immediately to prepare his master's meal, and on top of that he had to wait at table--and all that before he had had any food himself. He just went and did it, expecting nothing else. How unwilling we are for this! How quickly there are murmurings and bitterness in our hearts when that sort of thing is expected of us. But the moment we start murmuring, we are acting as if we had rights, and a bond-servant hasn't any!

Secondly, in doing this he must be willing not to be thanked for it. How often we serve others, but what selfpity we have in our hearts and how bitterly we complain that they take it as a matter of course and do not thank us for it. But a bond-servant must be willing for that. Hired servants may expect something, but not bond-servants.

And, thirdly, having done all this, he must not charge the other with selfishness. As I read the passage, I could not but feel that the master was rather selfish and inconsiderate. But there is no such charge from the bond-servant. He exists to serve the interests of his master and the selfishness or otherwise of his master does not come into it with him. But we? We can perhaps allow ourselves to be "put upon" by others, and are willing perhaps not to be thanked for what we do, but how we charge the other in our minds with selfishness! But that is not the place of a bond-servant. He is to find in the selfishness of others but a further opportunity to identify himself afresh with His Lord as the servant of all.

But there is a fourth step still to which we must go. Having done all that, there is no ground for pride or self-congratulation, but we must confess that we are unprofitable servants, that is, that we are of no real use to God or man in ourselves. We must confess again and again that "in us, that is in our flesh, there dwelleth no good thing," that, if we have acted thus, it is no thanks to us, whose hearts are naturally proud and stubborn, but only to the Lord Jesus, who dwells in us and who has made us willing.

The bottom of self is quite knocked out by the fifth and last step--the admission that doing and bearing what we have in the way of meekness and humility, we have not done one stitch more than it was our duty to do. God made man in the first place simply that he might be God's bond-servant. Man's sin has simply consisted in his refusal to be God's bond-servant. His restoration can only be, then, a restoration to the position of a bond-servant. A man, then, has not done anything specially meritorious when he has consented to take that position, for he was created and redeemed for that very thing.

This, then, is the Way of the Cross. It is the way that God's lowly Bond-servant first trod for us, and should not we, the bond-servants of that Bond-servant, tread it still? Does it seem hard and forbidding, this way down? Be assured, it is the only way up. It was the way by which the Lord Jesus reached the Throne, and it is the way by which we too reach the place of spiritual power, authority and fruitfulness. Those who tread this path are radiant, happy souls, overflowing with the life of their Lord. They have found "he that humbleth himself shall be exalted" to be true for them as for their Lord. Where before humility was an unwelcome intruder to be put up with only on occasions, she has now become the spouse of their souls, to whom they have wedded themselves for ever. If darkness and unrest enter their souls it is only because somewhere on some point they have been unwilling to walk with her in the paths of meekness and brokenness. But she is ever ready to welcome them back into her company, as they seek her face in repentance.

That brings us to the all-important matter of repentance. We shall not enter into more abundant life merely by resolving that we shall be humbler in the future. There are attitudes and actions which have already taken place and are still being persisted in (if only by our unwillingness to apologise for them) that must first be repented of. The Lord Jesus did not take upon Him the form of a bond-servant merely to give us an example, but that He might die for these very sins upon the cross, and open a fountain in His precious Blood where they can all be washed away. But that Blood cannot be applied to the sins of our proud heart until we have been broken in repentance as to what has already happened and as to what we already are. This will mean allowing the light of God to go through every part of our hearts and into every one of our relationships. It will mean that we shall have to see that the sins of pride, which God will show us, made it necessary for Jesus to come from heaven and die on the Cross that they might be forgiven. It will mean not only asking Him to forgive us but asking others too. And that will be humbling indeed. But as we crawl through the door of the broken ones we shall emerge into the light and glory of the highway of holiness and humility.

CHAPTER 9.

THE POWER OF THE BLOOD OF THE LAMB

The message and challenge of Revival, which is coming to many of us these days is searching in its utter simplicity. It is simply that there is only one thing in the world that can hinder the Christian's walking in victorious fellowship with God and his being filled with the Holy Spirit--and that is sin in one form or another. There is only one thing in the world that can cleanse him from sin with all that that means of liberty and victory--and that is the power of the Blood of the Lord Jesus. It is, however, most important for us that we should see what it is that gives the Blood of Christ its mighty power with God on behalf of men, for then we shall understand the conditions on which its full power may be experienced in our lives.

How many achievements and how many blessings for men the Scripture ascribes to the power of the Blood of the Lord Jesus! By the power of His Blood peace is made between man and God.[footnote 1: 1 Col. 1:20] By its power there is forgiveness of sins and eternal life for all who put their faith in the Lord Jesus. [footnote 2:Col.1:14; John 6:54] By the power of His Blood Satan is overcome. [footnote 3: Rev. 12:11] By its power there is continual cleansing from all sin for us.[footnote 4:1 John 1:7] By the power of His Blood we may be set free from the tyranny of an evil conscience to serve the living God.[footnote 5:Heb. 9:14] By its infinite power with God the most unworthy have liberty to enter the Holy of Holies of God's presence and live there all the day.[footnote 6:Heb. 10:19] We may well ask what gives the Blood its power!

To that question we need to link this other question--how may we experience its full power in our lives? Too often that precious Blood does not have its cleansing, peace-giving, life-giving, sin-destroying power in our hearts, and too often we do not find ourselves in God's presence and fellowship all the day.

Whence its Power?

The answer to the first question is suggested by the phrase in the book of Revelation which describes the Blood of Christ by the tender expression, "the Blood of the Lamb."[footnote 7: Rev.7:14] Not the Blood of the Warrior, but the Blood of the Lamb! In other words that which gives the precious Blood its power with God for men is the lamb-like disposition of the One who shed it and of which it is the supreme expression. The title "the Lamb" so frequently given to the Lord Jesus in Scripture is first of all descriptive of His work--that of being a sacrifice for our sin. When a sinning Israelite wanted to get right with God, it was the blood of a lamb (sometimes that of goat) which had to be shed and sprinkled on the altar. Jesus is the

Divine fulfilment of all those lambs that men offered--the Lamb of God that taketh away the sin of the world.[Footnoe 8:John 1:29] But the title the Lamb has a deeper meaning. It describes His character. He is the Lamb in that He is meek and lowly in heart,[footnote 9:Matt. 11:29] gentle and unresisting, and all the time surrendering His own will to the Father's[footnote 10:John 6:38] for the blessing and saving of men. Any one but the Lamb would have resented and resisted the treatment men gave Him. But He, in obedience to the Father[footnote 11:Phil. 2:8] and out of love for us, did neither. Men did what they liked to Him and for our sakes He yielded all the time. When He was reviled, He reviled not again. When He suffered, He threatened not. No standing up for His rights, no hitting back, no resentment, no complaining! How different from us! When the Father's will and the malice of men pointed to dark Calvary, the Lamb meekly bowed His head in willingness for that too. It was as the Lamb that Isaiah saw Him, when he prophesied, "He is brought as a Lamb to the slaughter, and as a sheep before her shearers is dumb, so He openeth not His mouth."[footnote 12:Is. 53:7] The scourging, the scoffing, the spitting, the hair plucked off from His cheeks, the weary last march up the Hill, the nailing and the lifting up, the piercing of His side and the flowing of His Blood--none of these things would ever have been, had He not been the Lamb. And all that to pay the price of my sin! So we see He is not merely the Lamb because He died on the Cross, but He died upon the Cross because He is the Lamb.

Let us ever see this disposition in the Blood. Let every mention of the Blood call to mind the deep humility and self-surrender of the Lamb, for it is this disposition that gives the Blood its wonderful power with God. Hebrews 9:14 for ever links the Blood of Christ with His self-offering to God, "how much more shall the Blood of Christ, who through the eternal Spirit offered Himself without spot to God ..." And it is this fact that bestows upon it its power with God for men. For this disposition has ever been of supreme value to God. Humility, lamb likeness, the surrender of our wills to God are what He looks for supremely from man. It was to manifest all this that God ever created the first man. It was his refusal to walk this path that constituted his first sin (and it has been the heart of sin ever since). It was to bring this disposition back to earth that Jesus came. It was simply because the Father saw this in Him that He could say, "My Son, in Whom I am well pleased." It was because the shedding of His Blood so supremely expressed this disposition that it is so utterly precious to God and so all-availing for man and his sin.

The Second Question.

We come now to the second question--how can we experience its full power in our lives? Our hearts surely tell us the answer, as we look on the Lamb, bowing His Head for us on Calvary--only by being willing to have the same disposition that ruled Him and by bending our necks in brokenness as He bowed His. Just as it is the disposition of the Lamb that bestows upon the Blood its power, so it is only as we are willing to be partakers of the same disposition of the Lamb, that we shall know its full power in our lives. And we may be partakers of His disposition,[footnote13:

Phil.2:5; 1 Cor.2:16] for it has been made transferable to us by His death. All the fruits of the Holy Spirit, mentioned in Galatians 5--love, joy, peace, long-suffering, gentleness, goodness, faith, meekness, self-control--what are they but the expressions of the lamb-like nature of the Lord Jesus, and the Holy Spirit wants to fill us with them. Let us never forget that the Lord Jesus, though exalted to the throne of God, is still the Lamb (the book of Revelation tells us that) and He wants to reproduce Himself in us.

Are We Willing?

But are we willing for this? There is a hard unyielding self, which stands up for itself and resists others, that will have to be broken, if we are to be willing for the disposition of the Lamb, and if the precious Blood is to reach us in cleansing power. We may pray long to be cleansed from some sin and for peace to be restored to our hearts, but unless we are willing to be broken on the point in question and be made a partaker of the Lamb's humility there, nothing will happen. Every sin we ever commit is the result of the hard unbroken self taking up some attitude of pride, and we shall not find peace through the Blood until we are willing to see the source of each sin and reverse the wrong attitude that caused it by a specific repentance, which will always be humbling. This means that we have not merely to try and make ourselves feel the humility of Jesus. We have only to walk in the light and be willing for God to reveal any sin that may be in our lives, and we shall find ourselves asked by the Lord to perform all sorts of costly acts of repentance and surrender, often over what we term small and trivial matters. But their importance can be gauged by what it costs our pride to put them right. He may show us a confession or apology that has to be made to someone or an act of restitution that has to be done.[footnote14:Matt. 5:23-24] He may show us that we must climb down over something and yield up our fancied rights in it (Jesus had no rights--have we then?). He may show us that we must go to the one who has done us a wrong and confess to him the far greater wrong of resenting it (Jesus never resented anything or anyone--have we any right to?). He may call us to be open with our friends that they know us as we really are, and thus be able to have true fellowship with us. These acts may well be humiliating and a complete reversal of our usual attitudes of pride and selfishness, but by such acts we shall know true brokenness and become partakers of the humility of the Lamb. As we are willing for this in each issue, the Blood of the Lamb will be able to cleanse us from all sin and we shall walk with God in white, with His peace in our hearts.

CHAPTER 10.

PROTESTING OUR INNOCENCE?

We have all become so used to condemning the proud self-righteous attitude of the Pharisee in the parable of the Pharisee and the Publican,[footnote1:Luke 18:9-14] that we can hardly believe that the picture of him there is meant to apply to us-- which only shows how much like him we really are. The Sunday School teacher was never so much a Pharisee, as when she finished her lesson on this parable with the words, "And now, children, we can thank God that we are not as this Pharisee!" In particular are we in danger of adopting the Pharisee's attitude, when God is wanting to humble us at the Cross of Jesus, and show us the sins in our hearts that are hindering personal revival.

God's Picture of the Human Heart.

We shall not understand the real wrong of the Pharisee's attitude, nor of our own, unless we view it against the background of what God says about the human heart. Said Jesus Christ, "From within, out of the heart of men, proceed evil thoughts, adulteries, fornications, murders, thefts, covetousness, wickedness, deceit, lasciviousness, an evil eye, blasphemy, pride, foolishness."[footnote 2: Mark 7:20-23] The same dark picture of the human heart is given us in Paul's letter to the Galatians, "The works of the flesh are manifest, which are these; adultery, uncleanness, lasciviousness, idolatry, witchcraft, hatred, variance, emulations, wrath, strife, divisions, parties, envyings, murders, drunkenness, revellings and such like."[footnote 3: Gal.5:19-21] What a picture! Jeremiah adds the same witness, "The heart is deceitful above all things (that is, it deceives the man himself, so that he does not know himself) and desperately wicked, who can know it?"[footnote4:Jer.17:9] Here then is God's picture of the human heart, the fallen self, "the old man,"[footnote5:Eph.4:22] as the Scripture calls it, whether it be in the unconverted or in the keenest Christian. It is hard to believe that these things can proceed from the heart of ministers, evangelists and Christian workers, but it is true. The simple truth is that the only beautiful thing about the Christian is Jesus Christ. God wants us to recognise that fact as true in our experience, so that in true brokenness and self-despair we shall allow Jesus Christ to be our righteousness and holiness and all in all--and that is victory.

Making God a Liar!

Now in face of God's description of the human heart, we can see what it was that the Pharisee did. In saying, "I thank Thee that I am not as other men are, extortioners, unjust, adulterers," he was protesting his innocence of the very things that God says are in every heart. He said in effect, "These things are doubtless true of other men--this Publican is even now confessing them--but, Lord, not of me!" And in so saying, he was making God a liar, for "if we say we have not sinned, we make Him a liar,"[footnote6:1 John 5:10] because He says we have! Yet I feel sure that he was perfectly sincere in what he said. He really did believe that he was innocent of these things. Indeed, he is ascribing his imagined innocence to God, saying, "I thank thee ..." God's word, however, still stood against him. But he just had not seen it. The "penny had not dropped!" If the Publican is beating upon his breast and confessing his sins, it is not because he has sinned worse than the Pharisee. It is simply that the Publican has seen that what God says is woefully true of him, and the Pharisee has not. The Pharisee still thinks that outward abstinence from certain sins is all that God requires. He has not yet understood that God looks, not on the outward appearance, but on the heart,[footnote7:1 Sam.16:7] and accounts the look of lust the equivalent of adultery,[footnote8:Matt.5:27-28] the attitude of resentment and hate the same as murder,[footnote9:1 John 3:15.] envy as actual theft, and the petty tyrannies in the home as wicked as the most extortionate dealings in the market.

How often have not we, too, protested our innocence on the many occasions when God has been convicting others, and when He has wanted to convict us too. We have said in effect, "These things may be true of others, but not of me!" and we may have said so quite sincerely. Perhaps we have heard of others who have humbled themselves and have rather despised them for the confessions they have had to make and the things they had to put right in their lives. Or perhaps we have been genuinely glad that they have been blessed. But, whichever it is, we don't feel that we have anything to be broken about ourselves. Beloved, if we feel we are innocent and have nothing to be broken about, it is not that these things are not there, but that we have not seen them. We have been living in a realm of illusion about ourselves. God must be true in all that He says about us. In one form or another, He sees these things expressing themselves in us (unless we have recognised them and allowed God to deal with them)--unconscious selfishness, pride and self-congratulation; jealousy, resentment and impatience; reserve, fears and shyness; dishonesty and deception; impurity and lust; if not one thing, then another. But we are blind to it. We are perhaps so occupied with the wrong the other man has done us, that we do not see that we are sinning against Christ in not being willing to take it with His meekness and lowliness. Seeing so clearly how the other man wants his own way and rights, we are blind to the fact that we want ours just as much; and yet we know there is something missing in our lives. Somehow we are not in vital fellowship with God. We are not spiritually crisp. Our service does not "crackle with the supernatural." Unconscious sin is none the less sin with God and separates us from Him. The sin in question may be quite a small thing, which God will so readily show us, if we are only willing to ask Him.

There is yet another error we fall into, when we are not willing to recognise the truth of what God says of the human heart. Not only do we protest our own innocence, but we often protest the innocence of our loved ones. We hate to see them being convicted and humbled and we hasten to defend them. We do not want them to confess anything. We are not only living in a realm of illusion about ourselves, but about them too, and we fear to have it shattered. But we are only defending them against God--making God a liar on their behalf, as we do on our own, and keeping them from entering into blessing, as we do ourselves.

Only a deep hunger for real fellowship with God will make us willing to cry to God for His all-revealing Light and to obey it when it is given.

Justifying God.

That brings us to the Publican. With all that God says about the human heart in our minds, we can see that his confession of sin was simply a justifying of God, an admission that what God said of him was true. Perhaps like the Pharisee, he used not to believe that what God said about man was really true of him. But the Holy Spirit has shown him things in his life which prove God right, and he is broken. Not only does he justify God in all that he has said, but he doubtless justifies God in all the chastening judgments God has brought upon him. Nehemiah's prayer might well have been his, "Howbeit Thou art just in all that is brought upon us; for Thou hast done right and we have done wickedly."[footnote10:Neh.9:33]

This is ever the nature of true confession of sin, true brokenness. It is the confession that my sin is not just a mistake, a slip, a something which is really foreign to my heart ("Not really like me to have such thoughts or do such things!"), but that it is something which reveals the real 'I'; that shows me to be the proud, rotten, unclean thing God says I am; that it really is like me to have such thoughts and do such things. It was in these terms that David confessed his sin, when he prayed, "Against Thee, Thee only, have I sinned and done this evil in Thy sight, that Thou mightest be justified when Thou speakest and be clear when Thou judgest."[footnote11:Psalm 51:4] Let us not fear then, to make such a confession where God convicts us that we must, thinking that it will "let Jesus down." Rather the reverse is true, for out of such confession God gets glory, for we declare Him to be right. This brings us to a new experience of victory in Christ, for it declares afresh, that "in me (that is, in my flesh), dwelleth no good thing,"[footnote12:Rom.7:18] and brings us to a place where we give up trying to make our incorrigible selves holy and where we take Jesus to be our holiness and His life to be our life.

Peace and Cleansing.

But the Publican did something more than justify God. He pointed to the sacrifice on the altar, and found peace with God and cleansing from sin, as he did so. That comes out in the literal meaning of the words which he uttered, "God be merciful to me, a sinner." In the Greek, the words mean literally, "God be propitiated to me, the sinner." The only way by which a Jew knew that God could be propitiated was by a sacrifice, and, in all probability, at that very hour the lamb for the daily burnt offering was being offered up on the altar in the temple.

With us it is the same. A man never comes to this position of brokenness, but God shows him the Divine Lamb on Calvary's Cross, putting away his sin by the shedding of His Blood. The God who declares beforehand what we are, provides beforehand for our sin. Jesus was the Lamb slain for our sins from the foundation of the world. In Him, who bore them in meekness, my sins are finished. And as I, in true brokenness, confess them, and put my faith in His Blood, they are cleansed and gone. Peace with God then comes into my heart, fellowship with God is immediately restored, and I walk with Him in white.

This simple way of being willing to justify God and see the power of the Blood to cleanse brings within our reach, as never before, a close walk with Jesus, a constant dwelling with Him in the Holy of Holies. As we walk with Him in the Light, He will be showing us all the time the beginnings of things which, if allowed to pass, will grieve Him and check the flow of His life in us--things which are the expression of that old proud self, for which God has nothing but judgment. At no point must we protest our innocence of what He shows us. All along we must be willing to justify Him and say, "Thou art right, Lord; that just shows what I am," and be willing to give it to Him for cleansing. As we do so, we shall find that His precious Blood is continuously cleansing us from sin, and that "the tide is being continuously healed at its beginning," and Jesus is continuously filling us with His Spirit. This demands that we must be men of "a humble and contrite spirit," that is, men who are willing to be shown the smallest thing. But such are the ones, God says, who "dwell with Him in the high and holy place,"[footnote13:Is.57:15] and who experience continuous revival.

There then is our choice--to protest our innocence and go down to our house, unblessed, dry of soul and out of touch with God. Or to justify God and to enter into peace, fellowship and victory through the Blood of Jesus.

1357487R00028

Made in the USA
San Bernardino, CA
12 December 2012